H is for Harvey

H is for Hugs
to Riley, Noah &
Asher!
♡ Julia Beasley

H is for Harvey

Written by Julie Beasley

Illustrated by Eduardo Martinez

Foreword by The Astros Foundation

TCU
Press

Fort Worth, Texas

Library of Congress Cataloging-in-Publication Data

Names: Beasley, Julie, 1974- author. | Martinez, Eduardo (Illustrator),
    illustrator.
Title: H is for Harvey / Julie Beasley ; illustrated by Eduardo Martinez.
Description: Fort Worth, Texas : TCU Press, [2018] | Audience: 005-010. |
    Audience: K-4. | "This book is dedicated to those who lost their lives to
    Hurricane Harvey, to those whose families, homes, and businesses were
    affected, to the millions of people in the US and around the world who
    have helped those affected by tragedy, and especially to those first
    responders who put their lives on the line for others every day."
Identifiers: LCCN 2018015520 | ISBN 9780875657059 (alk. paper)
Subjects: LCSH: Hurricane Harvey, 2017--Juvenile literature. |
    Hurricanes--Texas--Juvenile literature. | Disaster relief--Texas--Harris
    County--Juvenile literature. | Disaster relief--Texas--Houston--Juvenile
    literature. | Harris County (Tex.)--History--21st century--Juvenile
    literature. | Houston (Tex.)--History--21st century--Juvenile literature.
    | LCGFT: Picture books.
Classification: LCC QC945 .B43 2018 | DDC 363.34/922097641411--dc23
LC record available at https://urldefense.proofpoint.com/v2/url?u=https-
    3A__lccn.loc.gov_2018015520&d=DwIFAg&c=7Q-
    FWLBTAxn3T_E3HWrzGYJrC4RvUoWDrzTlitGRH_A&r=O2eiy819IcwTGuw-
    vrBGiVdmhQxMh2yxeggw9qlTUDE&m=P09Vhi _Y6aMU2AEd75qjkNsirlZbPmfkD6g1gs8FA
    68&s=vQ4OyZtKSzJ22jDeOAD4bcGB_qAawnSaCvklhTJp96M&e=

TCU Box 298300
Fort Worth, TX 76129

To order books, call 1.800.826.8911

This book is dedicated to those who lost their lives to Hurricane Harvey,
to those whose families, homes, and businesses were affected,
to the millions of people in the US and around the world
who have helped those affected by tragedy,
and especially to those first responders
who put their lives on the line for others every day.

Foreword

THE ASTROS
FOUNDATION

The 2017 season was one of the most memorable in Astros history, not only because the team won its first World Series Championship, but because of the strengthened bond between the team and the City of Houston in the wake of Hurricane Harvey. The incredible resilience, compassion, and heart that Houstonians displayed during and after the storm showed the world just how Houston Strong our city truly is.

The Astros were playing a three-game series in California against the LA Angels when Hurricane Harvey made landfall in Houston. When they were finally able to return home, the team decided to postpone their scheduled home game and went instead to volunteer and visit with those affected by Harvey at local shelters in downtown Houston. From that point through the end of the World Series, all Astros players and coaches wore Houston Strong patches on their jerseys as a constant reminder of what the fans and the city meant to them and the entire Astros organization.

The Astros Foundation, in coordination with Astros Owner and Chairman Jim Crane and ownership group, committed $4 million of aid for relief efforts throughout the Houston community in the immediate aftermath of Hurricane Harvey. Those relief efforts are ongoing, and, with your support, will continue to make a difference throughout Houston and the surrounding areas.

Congratulations, Julie, on your individual efforts to support the City of Houston and those impacted by Harvey. We appreciate your passion for this book, the proceeds of which will also benefit The Astros Foundation and its continued work throughout the Houston community as it rebuilds from Hurricane Harvey.

—The Astros Foundation
Houston, Texas
June 2018

s for **hurricane,** spinning wild
n the ocean. Harvey's its name,
tirring up the commotion.

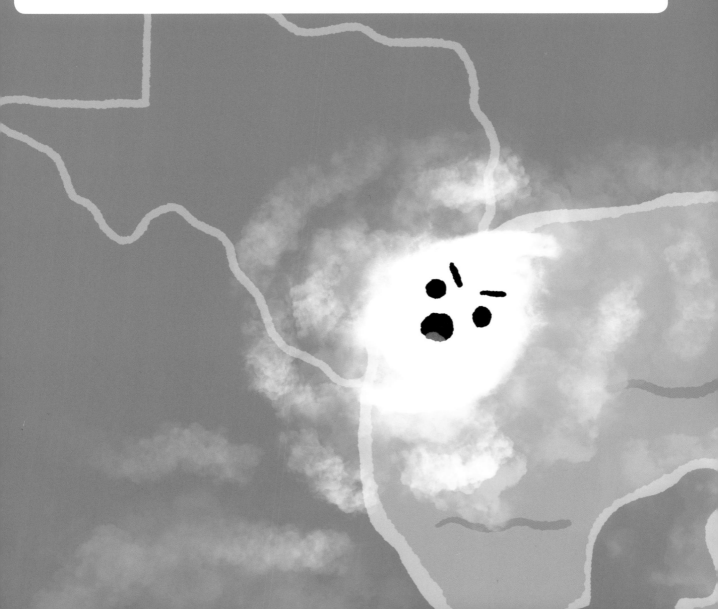

is for **hurry!** It's time to prepare.
Harvey hitting the coast—Texas, beware.

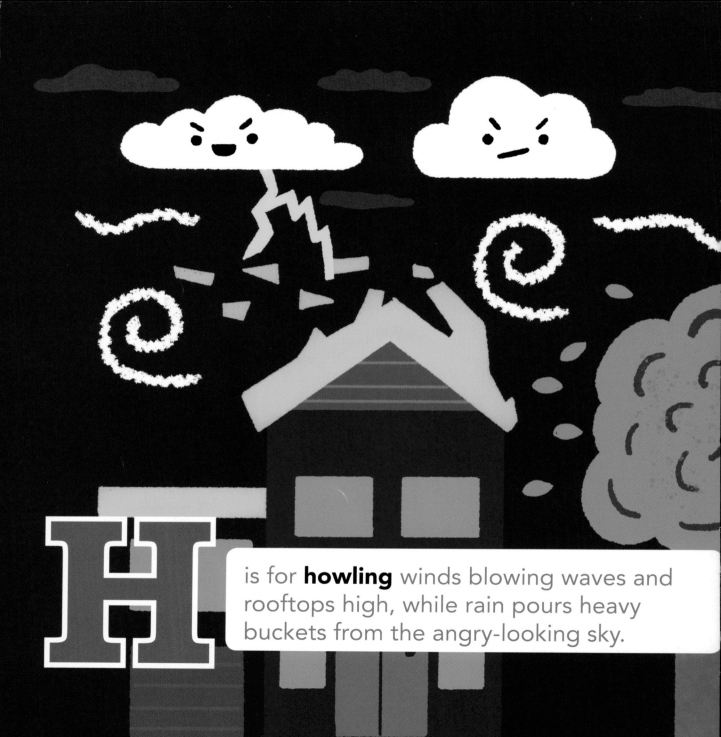

is for **howling** winds blowing waves and rooftops high, while rain pours heavy buckets from the angry-looking sky.

H is for **homes** and **highways** under water for miles and miles. From Texas town to Texas town, disaster wipes out happy smiles.

H is for **hurting** mothers, fathers, sisters, and brothers ... grandparents, aunts and uncles, neighbors, sons, and daughters ... Wading in rising waters ... Climbing higher ... Praying harder ...

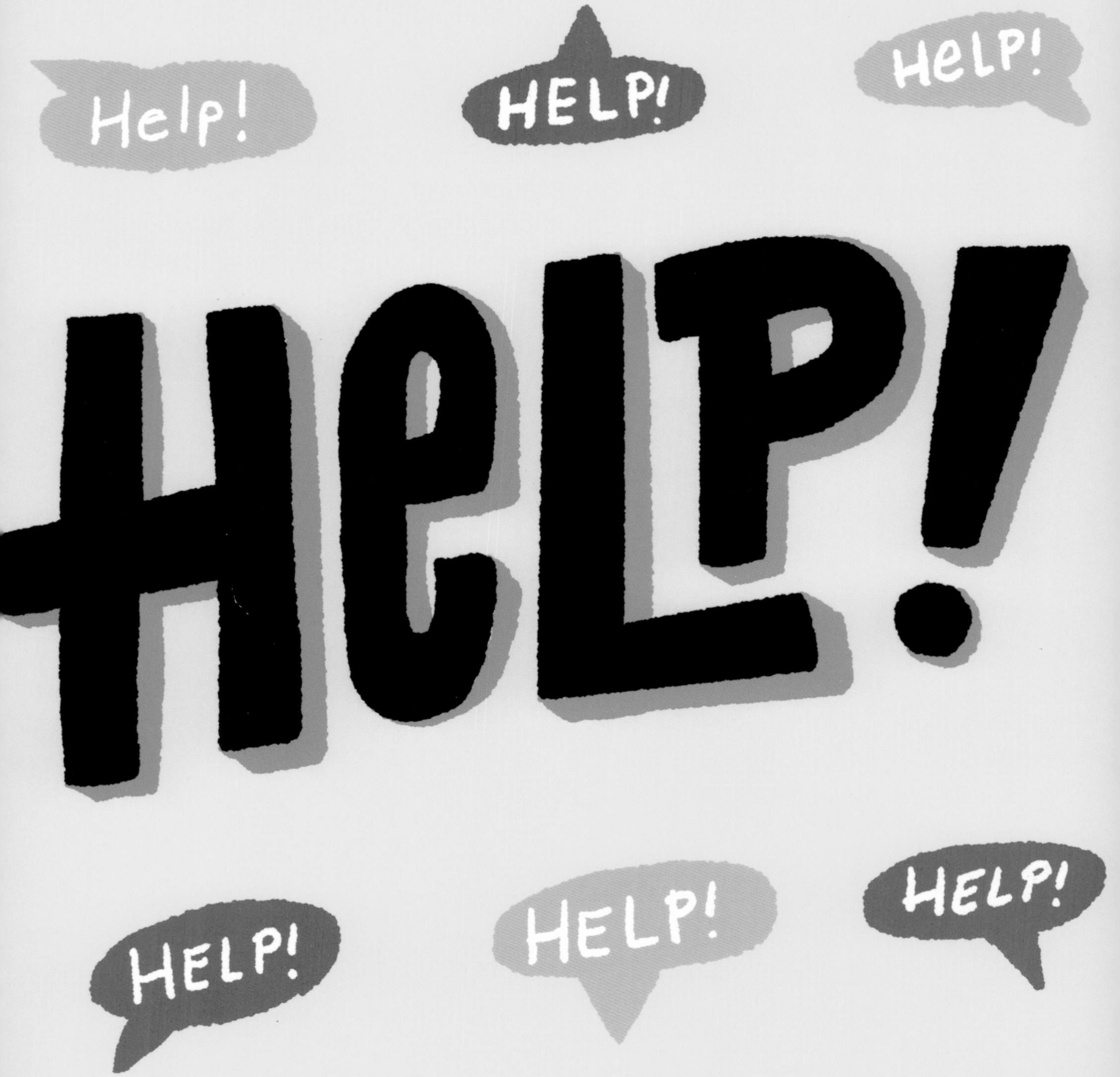
Help!
HELP!
HeLP!
HELP!
HELP!
HELP!
HELP!

H

is for **huddle,** it is time to make a plan. Let's help those harmed by Harvey just as fast as we can!

H

is for the **heroes,** the kind without a cape—
first responders helping people trapped by
water to escape.

H

is for **helicopters** swooping down from up above. Good Samaritans rescue others out of civic duty and love.

H

is for big **Humvees** and high-water vehicles, driven by Special Forces performing miracles.

H

is for **hospitals** working around the clock, facing countless hurdles but their care never stops.

H

is for **homeless** four-legged pets, rescued and cared for by volunteers and vets.

H is for **hugs** that evacuees need a lot, as shelters give tired humans a pillow and a cot.

H is for **hot** meals for those with no home or kitchen, helped by kindly neighbors and churches with a mission.

H is for **hashtags** found tweet after tweet. Social media requests for help down street after street.

#HOUSTONSTRONG

#HARVEY

#HARVEY2017

#HURRICAN

#TEXASSTRONG

#DISASTE

#HARVEYRESCUE

#SOSHOUSTON

H is for the **hammers** used to rebuild broken homes. Friends and strangers pitching in—no one needs to work alone!

H is for **hundreds** of thousands of hands reaching out from far and near. With drinking water, clothes, and food, or taking time to volunteer.

is for **healing,** a little more each day . . .
and human kindness shown from folks in places
far away.

H

is for **humongous** strength shown during devastation, with aid for the people of Texas from people across the nation.

H is for the **hope** that every morning will be better, with heartening proof that tragedy can bring our country close together.

H is for **How**

How long ago did Harvey happen?

▶ **Harvey made landfall near the Gulf Coast in Rockport, Texas, on August 25, 2017.**

https://weather.com/storms/hurricane/news/tropical-storm-harvey-forecast-texas-louisiana-arkansas
https://www.worldvision.org/disaster-relief-news-stories/hurricane-harvey-facts#strength

How long did Harvey last?

▶ **The extremely slow-moving hurricane hung around until August 30, when it made its final landfall in Louisiana. The impacts of Harvey lasted long after, however, because of the immense flooding.**

https://weather.com/storms/hurricane/news/tropical-storm-harvey-forecast-texas-louisiana-arkansas

How big was Harvey?

▶ **Hurricane Harvey was a Category 4 hurricane with 130-mph winds that affected some fifty Texas counties, including Harris County, the second largest county in the nation.**

https://www.worldvision.org/disaster-relief-news-stories/hurricane-harvey-facts#strength
https://weather.com/storms/hurricane/news/tropical-storm-harvey-forecast-texas-louisiana-arkansas
http://www.sandiegouniontribune.com/opinion/the-conversation/sd-hurricane-harvey-texas-flooding-displaces-thousands-20170828-htmlstory.html
https://www.houstonchronicle.com/news/houston-texas/houston/article/Harris-County-drops-to-No-2-nationally-in-11024290.p

How much water fell because of Harvey?

▶ **Thirty-three trillion gallons of water fell in Texas, Louisiana, Tennessee, and Kentucky. To date, this number is a US record for a single tropical storm. Houston, the country's fourth largest city, and its suburbs had more than fifty inches of rain over four days, flooding over a third of the Houston area.**

https://www.washingtonpost.com/news/capital-weather-gang/wp/2017/08/30/harvey-has-unloaded-24-5-trillion-gallons-of-water-on-texas-and-louisiana/?utm_term=.3960be6e1d69
http://www.nola.com/hurricane/index.ssf/2017/08/harvey_houston_30_percent_unde.html
https://www.worldvision.org/disaster-relief-news-stories/hurricane-harvey-facts#strength

How many people were affected by Harvey?

▶ **It is estimated that thirteen million people were affected by Harvey. Flooding forced 39,000 people out of their homes and into shelters, and approximately 200,000 homes were damaged or ruined.**

http://abcnews.go.com/US/hurricane-harvey-wreaks-historic-devastation-numbers/story?id=49529063
https://www.thebalance.com/hurricane-harvey-facts-damage-costs-4150087
https://globalnews.ca/news/3708870/hurricane-harvey-south-asian-floods

How much did Harvey damages cost?

▶ **With over $125 billion in damages, Harvey ranks as the second costliest hurricane ever to hit the US mainland.**

https://www.worldvision.org/disaster-relief-news-stories/hurricane-harvey-facts#strength

How was Harvey named?

▶ **The World Meteorological Organization creates a list of names that are in alphabetical order, alternating between masculine and feminine names.**

https://public.wmo.int/en/About-us/FAQs/faqs-tropical-cyclones/tropical-cyclone-naming
https://geology.com/hurricanes/hurricane-names.shtml

HOW CAN I HELP THOSE HURT BY HARVEY?

Buying this book is a good start. All royalties for H is for Harvey will benefit The Astros Foundation and will be used to directly support their ongoing Harvey relief efforts. Learn how you can donate by visiting Astros.com/donate.

All Hands Volunteers at Hands.org through its Texas Hurricane Recovery Program and the Rebuild Texas Fund at rebuildtx.org are two other organizations supporting Harvey relief efforts.

Even asking friends or family recovering from Hurricane Harvey how they are doing can go a long way!

Dear Letter H

Hi, how do you do? I bet your alphabet neighbors G and I are proud to be next to you. I must admit, H, I never thought you a letter to admire. I drew hearts and happy faces, no spelling required. Words like "hippopotamus" and "hieroglyphics" I found difficult, but now—I'm inspired! So I will write you proudly each day to salute you and all the things you start with and stand for—you hip, heroic, heck-of-an-alphabet soldier.

Hugs, Julie

H is for these helpful people who made this book possible!
A huge thank you to the following:

TCU Press
The Astros Foundation
Eduardo Martinez
Helaine Hudson
Seema Mir
Tobey Blanton Forney
Matt Foytlin

My husband Ian, children Elliott and Pippa,
parents Sue and Dennis, sisters Jenny and Melissa,
and in-laws for all the love and support.

Photo: Monica Jhunjhunwala

AUTHOR:
Julie Beasley is a creative director and copywriter who has worked at advertising agencies in Chicago, New York, and now Houston which she, her husband, and two children have called home since 2016. Born in Wisconsin and raised in Kansas and Indiana, Julie graduated with a BA in journalism and advertising from Ball State University.

ILLUSTRATOR:
Eduardo Martinez is an award-winning illustrator and designer. He served in the US Army for sixteen years before earning his bachelor of fine arts from the Art Institute of Houston in 2015. Born in San Luis Potosi, Mexico, Eduardo currently works at Rice University as a graphic designer. He lives in Houston with his wife and three children.

 is for **happy** ending.